© Warrior Made, All Right Reserved

All rights reserved. Printed in the United States of America. No part of this book my be used or reproduced in any manner whatsoever without written permission except in the case of brief quotations embodied critical articles or reviews.

This book is not intended as a substitute for the medical advice of physicians. The reader should regularly consult a physician in matters relating to his/her health and particularly with respect to any symptoms that may require diagnosis or medical attention.

Although the author and publisher have made every effort to ensure that the information in his book was correct at press time, the author and publisher do not assume and hereby disclaim any liability to any party for any loss, damage, or disruption caused by errors or omissions, whether such errors or omissions result from negligence, accident, or any other case.

The Author assumes no responsibility for errors or omissions that may appear in this publication. While all attempts have been made to verify information provided in this publication. The Author does not assume any responsibility for errors, inaccuracies or omissions. Any slights of people or organizations are unintentional.

Company names and product names mentioned in this document may be trademarks or registered trademarks of their respective companies and are hereby acknowledged.

For information contact;
c/o Warrior Made
PO Box 1499, Soquel CA 95073
WarriorMade.com

Book and Cover Design by Andrea Horowitt
Production Director Ben Chargin
Recipe Photos by Elisa Silva, Genevieve Rico
Introduction Edited by CD Johnson
Select Photos Taken by Irana Sumchenko
Editing Contributors Lauren Smith, Nina Moseley

Property of Warrior Made ISBN 9780997770353
First Edition August 2018
10 9 8 7 6 5 4 3 2 1

# KETO
## Sweet Treats

WITH ELISA SILVA

# CONTENTS

# INTRODUCTION

One of the biggest challenges I've ever seen anyone face is trying to change their life alone.

Making a big change by yourself can be one of the fastest ways to fail. That's why I'm so glad you decided to begin your body transformation journey with me today!

My name is Elisa, but my friends call me "Chef." I'm the head recipe coach over at WarriorMade.com which is a website created to help people, just like you and me, transform our bodies and lives. We achieve this by teaching you diet, exercise and lifestyle strategies to live a healthy, happy, and lean life.

One of the core beliefs at WarriorMade.com is that our society eats way too many sugars and carbohydrates, and one of the best ways to lose fat and reclaim your health is by eating a low carb or ketogenic diet. The good news is, the ketogenic diet is not as hard as you think. Plus, I'm here to walk with you through every step of your new keto lifestyle!

Before I do that though, I'd like to share something personal with you. You see, I wouldn't be here if it wasn't for my Mom. She was an incredible Chef who trained under some of the best culinary minds in California, and she taught me everything she knew about cooking. By the time I was a teenager, she had taught me how to make authentic dishes from places like Japan, Italy, Greece, and so many others.

The only trouble was, even though my Mom could create meals that people happily paid hundreds of dollars for, she struggled with her weight and more importantly, her health. As a young girl, I watched her battle with disordered eating. While my family and I would eat the incredible dinners she cooked for us, she seemed only to push food around her plate with a fork, never taking a bite. That was until I turned 14 and everything changed.

Her dietary habits were unsustainable and her body didn't know what to make of the food she was eating. This was the year my Mom was put into the hospital for the first time. She was never able to bring herself to eat the kinds of foods that would properly nourish her, and it took a severe toll on her health and our entire family. So, for months at a time, we would visit her in the hospital. Over the span of three years her health rapidly declined — until she passed away in May of 2003.

It was at this point, after the loss of my Mother, that I decided to take a stand and change my life. I had been left alone to figure life out — all because she never learned how to take control over what she ate and even more importantly, how to take care of herself.

I decided I would never again eat anything that could threaten my chance to love my children for as long as possible. From my experience, the freedom to live a healthy long life and to love my family for as long as I could was well worth any amount of effort food preparation could demand. So, from that point forward, healthy cooking became the key to unlocking my best possible life.

Fast forward 10 years: I now spend hours every week searching for the best recipes to feed myself and my family. I've researched every diet out there, read countless cookbooks, and made hundreds of failed recipes that sometimes, even my dog wouldn't eat!

Along the way, there has been only one type of diet that I've seen actively and consistently help people regain proper nourishment, find a healthy balance with food, and lose undesired weight. As I'm sure you already know (because you're reading this book), it's the ketogenic diet!

After I became really proficient as a keto/low-carb chef, my friends and family started asking me for healthy recipes constantly. Every day, I see how the recipes I adapt and create are changing peoples' lives. My friends and family all have slimmer waistlines, higher energy, deeper sleep, and feel better overall.

These recipes are so quick and easy that the people who use them notice that they have more time to spend on the things that really matter in life.

The thing is...I never thought about creating dessert recipes up front. And that was a problem because my friends and family love sweets!

My kids begged me every night for cookies or brownies, and I never knew what to say to them except, "No."

This was not good.

You see, having low carb and no sugar meals is great for you, but there isn't a person on the planet who can go without sweet treats for the rest of their life! That's torture! So, I set out to find a way to make my own dessert recipes that followed the guidelines of a ketogenic diet - things like ice cream, red velvet cake, snickerdoodles, and more.

The best part is that all the recipes are keto! You'll love these recipes just like my friends and family do, and you'll still get to enjoy the same benefits of eating a ketogenic diet all without sacrificing your favorite treats!

All my recipes are compiled into an amazing book I call Keto Sweet Treats. It will give you the secret to unlocking the most potential in your health and ensure that you are able to continue on the ketogenic diet, no matter what you're eating!

I'm glad you have this recipe book, and I hope it serves you as well as it's served me and the people I love.

*Elisa Silva*

Chef Elisa

For more of Chef Elisa's ketogenic recipes, visit WarriorMade.com

# CAKES & PIES

# ANGEL FOOD CAKE

PREP TIME 20 MINUTES | COOK TIME 35 MINUTES | SERVES 6

12 egg whites, room temperature

1 teaspoon cream of tartar

1 teaspoon vanilla extract

¾ cup super fine almond flour

¼ cup arrowroot powder

⅛ teaspoon sea salt

½ cup monk fruit sweetener

Calories per serving 81
Total fat 2g
Total carbohydrates 7g
Fiber 0g; *Net carbs 6g*
Protein 8g

## Directions

Preheat oven to 350°F. Line a round cake pan with parchment paper.

Combine the dry ingredients in a bowl and set aside.

In a large bowl, beat the egg whites with an electric mixer until frothy.

Add cream of tartar to the egg whites. Beat on high until stiff peaks form.

Reduce the speed of your mixer to low, and add the vanilla extract.

Fold the dry ingredients into the egg whites slowly.

Spoon the mixture into the cake pan and bake for 35 minutes.

Allow the cake to cool completely before serving.

# LEMON RICOTTA CAKE

PREP TIME 10 MINUTES | COOK TIME 50 MINUTES | SERVES 12

½ stick of butter, room temperature

½ cup granulated Swerve

1 cup whole milk ricotta cheese

4 large eggs

1 ½ tablespoons fresh lemon juice

Zest from 1 lemon

½ teaspoon almond extract

1 cup almond flour

4 tablespoons coconut flour

2 teaspoons baking powder

¼ teaspoon salt

Confectioners Swerve (optional)

---

Calories per serving 157
Total fat 13g
Total carbohydrates 5g
Fiber 2; *Net carbs 3g*
Protein 7g

## Directions

Preheat oven to 325°F. Line an 8-inch cake pan with parchment paper.

Cream together butter, almond extract, and granulated Swerve with an electric mixer.

Add ricotta cheese, lemon zest, and lemon juice and continue mixing.

Slowly add 1 egg at a time to the mixture, beating after each one to incorporate them separately.

Mix ⅓ of the dry ingredients at a time until thoroughly combined.

Spread the mixture evenly into the pan. Bake for 50 minutes or until a toothpick inserted into the cake comes out clean.

Allow to cool for 20 minutes. Remove from the pan and top with Confectioners Swerve, if desired, and serve!

Calories per serving 282
Total fat 27g
Total carbohydrates 11g
Fiber 8g; *Net carbs 3g*
Protein 6g

# CHOCOLATE ROLL CAKE

PREP TIME 25 MINUTES | COOK TIME 12 MINUTES | SERVES 10

## Cake:

- 1 cup almond flour
- 4 tablespoons butter
- 3 large eggs
- ¾ teaspoon xanthan gum
- ¼ cup unsweetened cocoa powder
- ¼ cup heavy cream
- ¼ cup sour cream
- ¼ cup monk fruit sweetener
- 1 teaspoon vanilla extract
- 1 teaspoon baking powder

## Filling:

- 8 ounces cream cheese
- 8 tablespoons butter
- ¼ cup sour cream
- ¼ cup monk fruit sweetener
- 1 teaspoon vanilla extract

## Directions

Preheat oven to 350°F. Line a baking sheet with parchment paper.

Combine dry cake ingredients in a bowl. Slowly add the wet ingredients, mixing until well combined.

Spread the dough evenly on the baking sheet and bake for 12 to 15 minutes.

While the cake is cooking prepare the filling. Mix all of the filling ingredients with an electric mixer until well combined.

Remove the cake from the oven and allow to cool slightly.

Spread the filling evenly over the cake. Carefully roll the cake into a tube.

Refrigerate for 1 hour before slicing and serving.

# COCONUT CAKE WITH VANILLA

## CREAM CHEESE FROSTING

PREP TIME 15 MINUTES | COOK TIME 20 MINUTES | SERVES 8

### Cake:

- ½ cup coconut flour
- 4 tablespoons full fat coconut milk
- 5 egg yolks
- ½ cup monk fruit sweetener
- ½ cup butter softened
- ½ teaspoon vanilla extract
- ¼ cup shredded unsweetened coconut
- ½ teaspoon baking powder
- Pinch of salt

## Directions

### Cake:

Preheat the oven to 400°F. Line two 9-inch cake pans with parchment paper, and grease lightly.

In a bowl, cream butter and monk fruit sweetener until thoroughly combined.

Add the egg yolks, vanilla extract and coconut milk and continue to mix.

Slowly add coconut flour, salt and baking powder.

In a separate bowl, whisk the egg whites until stiff peaks form.

Fold the egg whites into the coconut milk mixture, gently making sure to not over mix.

Pour the batter evenly into the cake pans. Bake for 20 minutes or golden brown.

Remove from the oven and allow to cool completely.

Frosting:

Beat together cream cheese, vanilla and monk fruit sweetener.

Add coconut milk to thin out slightly and mix until smooth.

Assembly:

Ensure cakes are cooled completely before frosting. Generously frost the top of one cake.

Place the second cake on top. Press down slightly to remove air bubbles in the frosting.

Frost the top and sides with remaining frosting.

Sprinkle additional shredded coconut on top and sides of the cake.

Slice and serve.

Frosting:

3 tablespoons full fat coconut milk

1 8 oz packet cream cheese, softened

2 tablespoons monk fruit sweetener

1 teaspoon vanilla extract

Calories per serving 344
Total fat 2g
Total carbohydrates 7g
Fiber 3g; *Net carbs 4g*
Protein 8g

# VANILLA POUND CAKE

PREP TIME 15 MINUTES | COOK TIME 50 MINUTES | SERVES 12

2 cups superfine almond flour

½ cup salted butter

1 cup granulated monk fruit sweetener

2 teaspoons baking powder

1 teaspoon vanilla extract

1 cup full-fat sour cream

2 ounces cream cheese

4 large eggs

---

Calories per serving 236
Total fat 24g
Total carbohydrates 6g
Fiber 2g; **Net carbs 4g**
Protein 7g

## Directions

Preheat oven to 350°F. Grease a 9-inch bundt pan.

In a large bowl, combine almond flour and baking powder.

Melt butter and cream cheese together in a pan over low heat, making sure not to burn the cream cheese.

Remove from heat and add monk fruit sweetener, vanilla extract and sour cream, stirring until well combined.

Slowly mix wet ingredients with dry ingredients.

Add eggs and mix until well combined.

Pour batter into pan and bake for 50 minutes or until a toothpick inserted into the cake comes out clean.

Allow cake to cool completely before removing it from the pan.

Slice and serve.

# CHOCOLATE SOUR CREAM CUPCAKES

PREP TIME 10 MINUTES | COOK TIME 20-25 MINUTES | SERVES 24

½ cup unsweetened cocoa powder

2 cups monk fruit sweetener

1 cup super-fine almond flour

½ cup coconut flour

3 teaspoons baking powder

1 cup black coffee

½ cup sour cream

½ cup unsalted butter

2 eggs

1 teaspoon vanilla extract

½ teaspoon sea salt

Calories per serving 93
Total fat 8g
Total carbohydrates 4g
Fiber 2g; **Net carbs 2g**
Protein 2g

## Directions

Preheat oven to 350°F. Line two muffin tins with cupcake liners.

In a large bowl, combine monk fruit sweetener, almond and coconut flours, cocoa powder, baking powder, vanilla extract and sea salt.

In a separate bowl, combine coffee, sour cream and butter.

Slowly add the coffee mixture to the dry ingredients and mix until well combined.

Add the eggs to the batter and mix until smooth.

Pour the batter into the cupcake liners.

Bake for 20 to 25 minutes or until a toothpick inserted into the cupcakes comes out clean.

Allow to cool before serving.

# ALMOND CAKE

PREP TIME 10 MINUTES | COOK TIME 40 MINUTES | SERVES 8-10

¾ cup almond flour

¼ cup unsweetened shredded coconut

¼ teaspoon almond extract

⅔ cup golden monk fruit sweetener

1 teaspoon vanilla extract

¼ teaspoon salt

4 eggs

½ cup softened butter

2 tablespoon sliced almonds

---

Calories per serving 230
Total fat 22g
Total carbohydrates 5g
Fiber 2g; *Net carbs 3g*
Protein 6g

## Directions

Preheat oven to 350°F.

Butter a 9-inch springform pan and line with parchment paper.

In a bowl mix the almond flour, shredded coconut, salt and monk fruit sweetener until combined thoroughly.

In a separate bowl, whisk together the eggs and vanilla extract.

Add softened butter and mix until completely combined.

Slowly add the wet ingredients into the dry ingredients. Mix until completely combined.

Pour the batter into the springform pan and spread evenly.

Sprinkle sliced almond flakes on top.

Bake for 40 minutes or until golden brown.

Once the cake is cooled, release the pan.

Slice and serve.

# CHOCOLATE SILK PIE

PREP TIME 25 MINUTES | COOK TIME 12 MINUTES | SERVES 12

## Crust:

3 cups almond flour

⅓ cup granulated Swerve

5 tablespoons butter, melted

¼ teaspoon sea salt

2 large eggs

1 teaspoon vanilla extract

¼ teaspoon arrowroot powder

## Filling:

16 ounces cream cheese, room temperature

4 tablespoons sour cream

4 tablespoons butter

1 tablespoon vanilla extract

½ cup granulated Swerve

½ cup cocoa powder

## Directions

Preheat oven to 350°F. Grease a 9-inch pie dish.

Add almond flour, arrowroot powder, and salt to a food processor and pulse a few times to mix. Add eggs, vanilla extract, and butter and process until well combined.

Spread the dough into evenly in the pie dish evenly.

Bake for 12 minutes, then remove and allow to cool while you make the filling.

To make the filling: mix the cream cheese, sour cream, butter, vanilla extract, cocoa powder and Swerve with an electric mixer until light and fluffy.

In a separate bowl, whip heavy cream and vanilla extract until soft peaks form. Slowly add in the Swerve and mix until well combined.

Fold the whipped cream into the filling mixture gently, spoonfuls at a time. Be careful to not over mix.

Pour the filling onto the pie crust and smooth the top with a spoon.

Cover and refrigerate for at least 3 hours. Once chilled, slice and serve.

Whipped Cream:

1 cup heavy cream

2 teaspoons granulated Swerve,

1 teaspoon vanilla extract

Calories per serving 432
Total fat 42g
Total carbohydrates 10g
Fiber 4g; *Net carbs 6g*
Protein 11g

# RED VELVET CAKE

PREP TIME 25 MINUTES | COOK TIME 40-45 MINUTES | SERVES 24

## Cake:

- 6 cups almond flour
- 1 ½ cup granulated Swerve
- ¾ cup coconut flour
- 4 tablespoons cocoa powder
- 3 teaspoons arrowroot powder
- 6 teaspoons baking powder
- 1 ½ teaspoons baking soda
- 1 ½ teaspoons salt
- 18 ounces Greek yogurt
- ¾ cup butter softened
- 9 large eggs
- 1 ½ teaspoons vanilla extract
- ¾ cup heavy cream
- 45 drops natural red food coloring

## Directions

Preheat oven to 325°F. Line 3 9-inch springform pans with parchment paper (or bake cakes one at a time).

Whisk together almond flour, coconut flour, cocoa powder, Swerve, baking powder, baking soda, arrowroot powder, and salt.

In another bowl, beat together Greek yogurt and butter. Slowly add the eggs until well combined.

Add almond flour mixture to egg mixture spoonfuls at a time, mixing well.

Mix in heavy cream.

Divide batter between prepared pans. Bake 40 to 45 minutes or until a toothpick inserted in center of the cakes comes out clean.

Allow to cool completely.

## Frosting:

Beat cream cheese and butter together until smooth. Beat in arrowroot powder, granulated Swerve, heavy cream and vanilla until combined fully.

## Assembly:

Place one layer of cake on serving platter and top with ½ to ¾ cup frosting, using a spatula to spread the frosting evenly. Repeat with remaining layers until all 3 layers are stacked. Smooth the remaining frosting over the top and sides of the cake.

Slice and serve.

## Frosting:

24 ounces cream cheese softened

½ cup butter softened

1 cup granulated swerve

3 tablespoon arrowroot powder

¾ cup heavy cream

1 ½ teaspoons vanilla extract

---

Calories per serving 462
Total fat 43g
Total carbohydrates 14g
Fiber 5g; *Net carbs 9g*
Protein 12g

# CARROT CAKE WITH CREAM CHEESE
## FROSTING

PREP TIME 30 MINUTES | COOK TIME 25 MINUTES | SERVES 12

### Cake:

- ½ cup monk fruit sweetener
- 5 tablespoons butter
- 4 large eggs
- 2 tablespoons heavy cream
- 1 teaspoon vanilla extract
- 1 ½ cups almond flour
- 2 tablespoons coconut flour
- 1 tablespoon baking powder
- 1 ½ teaspoon ground cinnamon
- 1 teaspoon ground ginger
- ¼ teaspoon ground nutmeg
- ½ cup shredded carrot
- ¼ teaspoon salt

### Directions

Preheat the oven to 350°F. Line the bottom of a 9-inch cake pan with parchment paper

Using an electric mixer, beat together monk fruit sweetener and butter until fluffy.

Add eggs, heavy cream and vanilla extract.

Slowly add almond flour, coconut flour, spices, salt and baking powder and mix well.

Fold in the shredded carrot with a rubber spatula and mix just until the carrot is incorporated.

Pour batter into cake pan. Bake for 20 to 25 minutes or until a toothpick inserted into the center of the cake comes out clean.

Allow to cool completely before frosting.

## Frosting:

Mix cream cheese and butter with an electric mixer until fluffy.

Add the Confectioners Swerve, heavy cream, and vanilla extract. Mix until smooth.

Remove cake from pan, frost, and serve.

## Frosting:

4 ounces cream cheese, room temperature

2 tablespoons butter, room temperature

1 teaspoon vanilla extract

1 tablespoon heavy cream

¼ cup Confectioners Swerve

Calories per serving 225
Total fat 20g
Total carbohydrates 6g
Fiber 2g; *Net carbs 4g*
Protein 6g

# NO-BAKE CHEESECAKE

## WITH CHOCOLATE GANACHE

PREP TIME 2 HOURS | SERVES 4

### Cheesecake:

4 ounces cream cheese

2 tablespoons sour cream

¼ cup heavy whipping cream

¼ cup stevia or monk fruit sweetener

### For the ganache:

2 ounces unsweetened baking chocolate

½ cup heavy cream

Splash of water

Calories per serving 260
Total fat 27g
Total carbohydrates 6g
Fiber 2g; *Net carbs 4g*
Protein 5g

### Directions

Using a hand mixer, mix together the cream cheese, sour cream, heavy cream, and sweetener.

Spoon some of the filling into cupcake molds and place in the freezer for 1 to 2 hours.

While the mixture is setting in the freezer, melt the unsweetened baking chocolate over a double boiler. Slowly add the heavy cream to the chocolate and mix until thoroughly combined.

Lastly add a splash of water and mix until you get a thick liquid-like consistency.

Pour the ganache over the top of the frozen cheesecakes and serve.

# CHOCOLATE ALMOND BUTTER PIE

PREP TIME 25 MINUTES | COOK TIME 30 MINUTES | SERVES 12

## Crust:

¾ cup coconut flour

2 tablespoons arrowroot powder

½ cup coconut oil

½ cup water

⅛ teaspoon salt

## Filling:

2 ounces unsweetened chocolate

1 can full-fat coconut milk

1 ¼ cups almond butter

½ teaspoon monk fruit sweetener

---

Calories per serving 158
Total fat 14g
Total carbohydrates 8g
Fiber 4g; *Net carbs 4g*
Protein 2g

## Directions

Preheat oven to 350°F. Grease a 9-inch pie dish.

In a bowl, melt together coconut oil and water. Slowly stir in the arrow root powder until a gel begins to form. Stir in the coconut flour and salt. Allow it to sit until all of the liquid is absorbed.

Take the dough and press it into the pie dish. Poke holes in the bottom of the crust with a fork to allow the air to escape during baking. Bake for 30 minutes.

To make the filling, melt the chocolate and add to a food processor. Add the remaining ingredients and blend until thoroughly combined.

Allow crust to cool slightly, then pour the filling into the crust.

Chill in the refrigerator for at least 6 hours, or overnight.

Slice and serve.

Calories per serving 194
Total fat 16g
Total carbohydrates 8g
Fiber 3g; *Net carbs 5g*
Protein 5g

# PUMPKIN PIE

PREP TIME 10 MINUTES | COOK TIME 50 MINUTES | SERVES 12

Crust:

2 cups almond flour

3 egg yolks

2 tablespoons butter, softened

2 tablespoons heavy cream

¼ teaspoon salt

Filling:

15 ounces organic pumpkin

1 tablespoon granulated Swerve

1 ½ teaspoons ground cinnamon

½ teaspoon ground nutmeg

¼ teaspoon ground cloves

3 eggs

⅔ cup heavy cream

½ teaspoon arrowroot powder

## Directions

Preheat oven to 350°F. Grease a 9-inch pie dish lightly and set aside.

In a food processor, pulse all the crust ingredients until a dough forms.

Press dough into pie dish starting at the bottom and working up the sides.

Bake for 10 minutes., Allow to cool while you make the filling.

Beat eggs, pumpkin, granulated Swerve, cinnamon, nutmeg and cloves with an electric mixer.

Add heavy cream. Mix until well combined.

Pour filling into pie crust and bake for 30 to 40 minutes.

Allow pie to cool completely, slice, and serve.

# VANILLA BIRTHDAY CAKE

## WITH CREAM CHEESE FROSTING

**PREP TIME 20 MINUTES | COOK TIME 1 HOUR | SERVES 24**

### Cake:

3 cups almond flour

½ cup coconut flour

1 cup granulated Swerve

½ cup full-fat coconut milk

1 tablespoon vanilla extract

8 large eggs

¼ teaspoon salt

1 ½ tablespoons baking powder

Pinch of salt

### Directions

**Cake:**

Preheat oven to 350°F. Line the bottom of 9-inch round springform pan with parchment paper (or three of the same pans, if you have them).

Beat in the eggs with a hand mixer. Add coconut milk, Swerve, salt and vanilla extract.

Slowly add in the almond flour, coconut flour, and baking powder and mix until well combined.

Pour of the cake batter into the pan and bake for 18 to 22 minutes until the top is slightly golden brown. Repeat with remaining batter until you have 3 separate cake layers.

Frosting:

While cake is baking, prepare your frosting.

Beat all frosting ingredients until smooth.

Assembly:

Allow cakes to cool completely before assembling. Once cooled, place one cake on a serving dish. Top with a layer of cream cheese frosting, then stack the next layer on top. Repeat. Use the remaining frosting to cover the top and sides of the cake.

Slice and serve.

Frosting:

32 ounces cream cheese, room temperature

⅓ cup butter, room temperature

⅔ cup Confectioners Swerve sweetener

1 teaspoon vanilla extract

Calories per serving 299
Total fat 28g
Total carbohydrates 13g
Fiber 3g; *Net carbs 8g*
Protein 8g

# NEW YORK-STYLE CHEESECAKE

PREP TIME 2 HOURS | COOK TIME 40 MINUTES | SERVES 12

## Crust:

1 ½ cups almond flour

½ cup melted butter

2 tablespoons granulated Swerve

¾ teaspoon ground cinnamon

⅛ teaspoon salt

## Filling:

3 cups cream cheese

2 cups full-fat sour cream

3 large eggs

4 tablespoons granulated Swerve

1 teaspoon vanilla extract

---

Calories per serving 447
Total fat 44g
Total carbohydrates 7g
Fiber 2g; **Net carbs 6g**
Protein 10g

## Directions

Preheat oven to 300°F. Line the bottom of an 9-inch springform pan with parchment paper.

Mix almond flour, melted butter, Swerve, salt, and cinnamon until well combined.

Pour mixture into the bottom of springform pan and press down evenly to create the crust.

Bake for 10 minutes until golden brown. Remove from oven and allow to cool while you make the filling.

Mix eggs, granulated Swerve, cream cheese, sour cream and vanilla extract with an electric mixer until well combined.

Pour the filling over the cooled crust.

Bake for 30 minutes. Remove and allow to cool completely.

Once cooled, refrigerate for at least 6 hours.

Release springform pan, slice, and serve.

# TRES LECHES CAKE

PREP TIME 20 MINUTES | COOK TIME 40 MINUTES | SERVES 12

## Cake:

½ cup unsalted butter, softened

⅔ cup monk fruit sweetener

1 ¼ cups almond flour

¼ teaspoon arrowroot powder

¼ teaspoon salt

2 teaspoons baking powder

3 large eggs

1 teaspoon vanilla extract

¼ cup heavy cream

1 cup full fat coconut milk

Liquid stevia to taste (about 5 drops)

## Directions

Preheat oven to 325°F. Grease a 9-inch round cake pan.

Combine almond flour, arrowroot powder, salt, and baking powder.

In a separate bowl, cream together butter, vanilla extract, and monk fruit sweetener using an electric mixer until light and fluffy.

Add eggs and heavy cream. Beat until well combined.

Slowly add the dry ingredients until you have a smooth batter.

Pour the batter into cake pan and bake for 30 to 40 minutes or until a toothpick inserted into the cake comes out clean.

Allow to cool for 15 minutes.

Carefully turn out the cake onto a serving plate.

In a small bowl, mix together coconut milk and liquid stevia.

Pour evenly over the cake.

To prepare the whipped cream, whip all of the ingredients in a bowl until stiff peaks form.

Top the cake with whipped cream, slice, and serve.

Whipped cream topping:

½ cup heavy cream

½ teaspoon vanilla extract

Liquid stevia to taste (about 5 drops)

---

Calories per serving 224
Total fat 21g
Total carbohydrates 4g
Fiber 1g; *Net carbs 3g*
Protein 5g

# CHOCOLATE LAYER CAKE

PREP TIME 15 MINUTES | COOK TIME 35 MINUTES | SERVES 24

## Cake:

2 ¼ cups almond flour

¾ cup cocoa powder

⅔ cup granulated monk fruit sweetener

6 ounces full-fat Greek yogurt, room temperature

½ cup butter, softened

5 large eggs

⅔ cup full-fat coconut milk

1 tablespoon instant coffee

2 teaspoons baking powder

1 teaspoon baking soda

1 teaspoon arrowroot powder

½ cup vanilla whey protein powder

½ teaspoon salt

## Directions

Preheat oven to 325°F. Line 2 8-inch cake pans with parchment paper and grease the parchment paper lightly.

Whisk together almond flour, cocoa powder, protein powder, monk fruit sweetener, instant coffee, baking powder, baking soda, arrowroot powder and salt.

In another bowl, beat together Greek yogurt and butter. Slowly add the eggs until well combined.

Add almond flour mixture to egg mixture spoonfuls at a time, mixing well.

Mix in coconut milk.

Divide batter between prepared pans. Bake 30 to 35 minutes or until a toothpick inserted in center of the cakes comes out clean. Let cool in the pans 10 minutes, and then turn out onto wire racks to cool completely.

Once cool, use a large serrated knife and cut each layer in half horizontally to create 4 layers total.

Beat the frosting ingredients with an electric mixer until smooth.

Place one layer of cake on serving platter and top with ½ to ¾ cup frosting, using a spatula to spread the frosting evenly. Repeat with remaining layers until all 4 layers are stacked. Smooth the remaining frosting over the top and sides of the cake.

Chill in refrigerator for at least an hour before slicing.

Sour cream frosting:

¾ cup unsweetened cocoa powder

3 cups granulated Swerve

2 teaspoons vanilla extract

¾ cup salted butter

¾ cup sour cream

3 tablespoons arrow root powder

Calories per serving 178
Total fat 16g
Total carbohydrates 12g
Fiber 3g; *Net carbs 9g*
Protein 5g

# NO-BAKE KEY LIME CHEESECAKE

PREP TIME 10 MINUTES | SERVES 12

## Crust:

2 cups almond flour

⅓ cup salted butter

3 tablespoons granulated Swerve sweetener

## Filling:

2 medium ripe avocados

12 ounces cream cheese, room temperature

4 limes

1 cup granulated Swerve

1 teaspoon vanilla extract

Calories per serving 304
Total fat 29g
Total carbohydrates 10g
Fiber 5g; **Net carbs 5g**
Protein 7g

## Directions

Line the bottom of a 9-inch pie dish with parchment paper.

To make the crust, combine almond flour, butter, and Swerve with an electric mixer.

Press the dough into the bottom of the pie dish.

For the filling, combine the cream cheese, granulated Swerve, vanilla extract, lime zest, and lime juice from all 4 limes in a food processor. Blend until the filling is smooth.

Spread the filling into the pie dish evenly.

Refrigerate for at least two hours or until the pie is firm.

Slice and enjoy.

Calories per serving 151
Total fat 12g
Total carbohydrates 7g
Fiber 4g; *Net carbs 3g*
Protein 5g

# CHOCOLATE POUND CAKE

¾ cups coconut flour

½ cup monk fruit sweetener

1/4 cup unsweetened cocoa powder

1 teaspoon baking powder

½ teaspoon baking soda

½ teaspoon instant coffee

6 large eggs

½ teaspoon vanilla extract

2 teaspoons apple cider vinegar

1 stick of butter

1 ounce unsweetened baking chocolate

½ teaspoon salt

¼ teaspoon arrowroot powder

## Directions

Preheat oven to 350°F. Line a loaf pan with parchment paper.

Chop the baking chocolate with a sharp knife and set aside.

Melt butter and chocolate in a saucepan over low heat, stirring continuously until melted completely.

In a bowl, mix all of your dry ingredients, and slowly add vanilla extract, eggs, apple cider vinegar.

Add the melted chocolate to cake mixture. Mix until well combined.

Quickly pour the batter into loaf pan and tap the bottom of the pan to get rid of any air bubbles.

Bake for 20 to 30 minutes until a knife inserted into the center of the cake comes out clean.

Allow the cake to cool before removing it from the pan.

Slice and serve.

# COOKIES

# GINGERSNAP COOKIES

PREP TIME 10 MINUTES | COOK TIME 17 MINUTES | MAKES 12

1 ¼ cup almond flour

¼ cup butter

4 tablespoons monk fruit sweetener

2 tablespoons water

¼ teaspoon ground allspice

1 teaspoon ground ginger

¼ teaspoon ground cloves

½ teaspoon ground cinnamon

¼ teaspoon salt

---

Calories per serving 105
Total fat 9g
Total carbohydrates 3g
Fiber 1g; *Net carbs 2g*
Protein 3g

## Directions

Cream the butter and monk fruit sweetener together until smooth.

Slowly add the almond flour, spices, salt and water, mixing until well combined.

Roll the dough into a ball and refrigerate for an hour.

Preheat oven to 325°F. Line a baking sheet with parchment paper.

Roll the dough out to about ¼-inch thick. Cut with a cookie cutter and place on baking sheet.

Bake for 7 minutes or until golden brown.

Turn the oven off and leave cookies in the oven for an additional 10 minutes to crisp up.

Allow cookies to cool completely on a wire rack and serve.

# NOT YOUR AVERAGE KETO COOKIE

PREP TIME 10 MINUTES | COOK TIME 15-20 MINUTES | MAKES 20

⅓ cup coconut oil

½ cup ghee

2 eggs

1 teaspoon vanilla extract

¾ cup stevia or monk fruit sweetener

½ teaspoon baking soda

¼ teaspoon cream of tartar

½ teaspoon salt

3 cups almond flour

---

Calories per serving 189
Total fat 17g
Total carbohydrates 5g
Fiber 2g; *Net carbs 3g*
Protein 4g

## Directions

Line a baking sheet with parchment paper and preheat the oven to 350°F.

In a medium sized bowl, using a hand mixer, mix the coconut oil and ghee.

Add the sweetener, baking soda, cream of tartar and salt to the same bowl. Mix until well incorporated.

Add the almond flour 1 cup at a time and mix with the hand mixer.

Form the dough into balls and lightly press down. Place on a cookie sheet (don't make the balls too big because they will spread during cooking baking).

Bake the cookies for 15 to 20 minutes, or until the cookies are golden brown.

Remove from the oven and allow them to cool before serving.

# SNICKERDOODLE COOKIES

PREP TIME 5 MINUTES | COOK TIME 12-15 MINUTES | MAKES 16

## Cookies:

- 2 cups superfine almond flour
- ½ cup salted butter, softened
- ½ teaspoon vanilla extract
- ½ teaspoon baking soda
- ¾ cup golden monk fruit sweetener

## Coating:

- 2 tablespoons golden monk fruit sweetener
- 1 ½ teaspoons ground cinnamon

---

Calories per serving 136
Total fat 12g
Total carbohydrates 3g
Fiber 3g; *Net carbs 2g*
Protein 3g

## Directions

Preheat oven to 350°F. Line a baking sheet with parchment paper.

Mix the cookie ingredients in a large bowl until thoroughly combined.

Form the dough into 16, 1 ½-inch balls

Combine the cinnamon and monk fruit sweetener in a medium-sized dish.

Roll the balls in the mixture until coated completely.

Place on the baking sheet and flatten slightly. Bake for 15 minutes

Allow to cool slightly before serving.

# OUTRAGEOUS CHOCOLATE COOKIES

PREP TIME 10 MINUTES | COOK TIME 12-15 MINUTES | MAKES 12

1 ¼ cups almond butter

2 large eggs

⅔ cup unsweetened cocoa powder

⅓ cup monk fruit sweetener

¼ teaspoon salt

½ teaspoon vanilla extract

---

Calories per serving 34
Total fat 2g
Total carbohydrates 3g
Fiber 2g; *Net carbs 1g*
Protein 2g

## Directions

Preheat oven to 320°F. Line a cookie sheet with parchment paper.

Place ingredients in a food processor. Blend until combined.

Form dough into 12 balls and place them on the baking sheet.

Flatten each ball by pressing down with a fork until about ½-inch thick.

Bake for about 12 minutes or until baked all the way through.

Allow to cool completely before serving.

Store in an airtight container for up to 5 days or freeze.

# CREAM CHEESE COOKIES

PREP TIME 10 MINUTES | COOK TIME 15 MINUTES | MAKES 24

¼ cup butter

2 ounces full fat-cream cheese

¾ cup monk fruit sweetener

1 large egg (white only)

2 teaspoons vanilla extract

3 cups almond flour

1 teaspoon lemon juice

¼ teaspoon sea salt

---

Calories per serving 112
Total fat 9g
Total carbohydrates 3g
Fiber 2g; **Net carbs 2g**
Protein 4g

## Directions

Preheat oven to 350°F. Line a baking sheet with parchment paper.

In a large bowl beat together butter, cream cheese, lemon juice, salt, and monk fruit sweetener, until it has reached a fluffy consistency.

Separate the egg and add the egg white and vanilla extract.

Slowly add in almond flour while continuing to mixing until combined thoroughly.

Form dough into about 1½-inch balls and set them on the baking sheet. Flatten slightly.

Bake for about 15 minutes until the edges are lightly golden.

Allow to cool completely before serving.

# ALMOND RICOTTA COOKIES

PREP TIME 10 MINUTES | COOK TIME 15-18 MINUTES | MAKES 24

2 cups almond flour

1 teaspoon baking powder

½ teaspoon baking soda

½ finely chopped almonds

½ cup butter

⅔ cup monk fruit sweetener

1 egg

⅔ cup full fat ricotta cheese

1 teaspoon almond extract

Calories per serving 105
Total fat 9g
Total carbohydrates 2g
Fiber 1g; *Net carbs 1g*
Protein 3g

### Directions

Preheat oven to 350°F. Line a baking sheet with parchment paper.

Mix together the wet ingredients.

In a separate bowl, combine all of the dry ingredients. Slowly add the dry ingredients to the wet ingredients until a dough forms.

Drop spoonfuls of cookie dough onto the baking sheet.

Bake for 15 to 18 minutes until lightly browned.

Allow to cool completely before serving.

# COCONUT MACAROONS

PREP TIME 15 MINUTES | COOK TIME 8 MINUTES | MAKES 10

¼ cup superfine almond flour

½ cup shredded unsweetened coconut

2 tablespoons monk fruit sweetener

½ tablespoon almond extract

1 tablespoon coconut oil

3 egg whites

⅛ teaspoon salt

---

Calories per serving 50
Total fat 4g
Total carbohydrates 1g
Fiber 1g; **Net carbs 1g**
Protein 2g

## Directions

Preheat oven to 400°F. Line a baking sheet with parchment paper.

In a bowl mix almond flour, shredded coconut, salt and monk fruit sweetener.

Melt coconut oil in a saucepan over a medium heat. Remove from heat and add almond extract.

Slowly add the melted coconut oil to the flour mixture. Mix until well combined.

In a separate bowl, whisk the egg whites until stiff peaks form.

Fold the egg whites into the flour mixture slowly, making sure not to over mix.

Drop spoonfuls of the mixture onto the cookie sheet. Bake for 8 minutes or until golden brown.

Allow to cool before removing from the baking sheet.

# CHOCOLATE ALMOND BUTTER

## NO-BAKE COOKIES

PREP TIME 10 MINUTES | MAKES 10

½ cup creamy almond butter

3 tablespoons cream cheese, softened

2 tablespoons salted butter, melted

1 teaspoon vanilla extract

2 tablespoons unsweetened cocoa powder

2 tablespoons Confectioners Swerve

¾ cup unsweetened shredded coconut

½ cup chopped almonds

**Directions**

Line a baking sheet with parchment paper.

Combine the almond butter and cream cheese in a large bowl. Mix until smooth.

Add butter, vanilla extract, cocoa powder and Confectioners Swerve. Mix until well combined.

Using a rubber spatula, fold in the coconut and chopped almonds.

Drop 1½-2-inch spoonfuls onto the baking sheet.

Chill for 10 minutes in freezer before serving.

Calories per serving 185
Total fat 17g
Total carbohydrates 9g
Fiber 4g; *Net carbs 5g*
Protein 5g

# COCONUT ALMOND CRISPS

PREP TIME 10 MINUTES | COOK TIME 8-12 MINUTES | MAKES 12

¼ cup butter

⅓ cup monk fruit sweetener

2 teaspoons sugar free maple syrup

¼ teaspoon arrowroot powder

¼ cup superfine almond flour

6 tablespoons unsweetened shredded coconut

½ teaspoon vanilla extract

---

Calories per serving 72
Total fat 7g
Total carbohydrates 2g
Fiber 1g; **Net carbs 1g**
Protein 1g

## Directions

Move oven rack to top of oven and preheat oven to 350°F. Line 2 baking sheets with parchment paper.

Combine butter, monk fruit sweetener, and maple syrup in a saucepan over medium heat. Stir frequently, until sweetner is dissolved and bubbles start to appear.

Remove from heat and add arrowroot powder. Whisk vigorously to combine. Stir in almond meal, shredded coconut and vanilla extract.

Drop teaspoons of batter onto the baking sheets. Press the cookies down with the bottom of a cup to flatten slightly.

Bake for 8 to 12 minutes, one sheet at a time, until the cookies have spread and the edges are dark golden.

Allow to cool completely and harden on baking sheet.

Store in an airtight container.

# CHOCOLATE ALMOND BUTTER
## BACON COOKIES

PREP TIME 15 MINUTES | COOK TIME 10 MINUTES | MAKES 12

6 slices bacon

1 cup chunky almond butter

1 cup golden monk fruit sweetener

1 large egg

½ cup unsweetened organic cocoa powder

1 ½ teaspoons vanilla extract

1 teaspoon baking soda

Calories per serving 199
Total fat 17g
Total carbohydrates 7g
Fiber 2g; **Net carbs 2g**
Protein 8g

### Directions

Preheat oven to 350°F. Line a baking sheet with parchment paper.

Cook bacon until crispy, crumble and set aside.

In a large mixing bowl, combine egg, almond butter, and monk fruit sweetener.

Add cocoa powder, baking soda, bacon crumbles, and vanilla extract, mixing until well combined.

With your hands form the dough into 12 equal-sized balls.

Place each ball on the baking sheet and flatten slightly.

Bake for 10 minutes.

Allow to cool completely before serving.

# ALMOND MERINGUE COOKIES

PREP TIME 10 MINUTES | COOK TIME 40 MINUTES | MAKES 10

4 large egg whites

¼ teaspoon cream of tartar

½ teaspoon almond extract

3 tablespoons confectioners Swerve

⅛ teaspoon salt

3 tablespoons arrowroot powder

Sliced almonds (optional)

---

Calories per serving 10
Total fat 0g
Total carbohydrates 5g
Fiber 0g; **Net carbs 5g**
Protein 1g

## Directions

Preheat oven to 210°F. Line a baking sheet with parchment paper.

Pour egg whites into a bowl and add the cream of tartar.

Whisk the egg whites with an electric mixer until frothy.

Add almond extract, salt, and half of the Confectioners Swerve.

Mix on high and slowly add the Confectioners Swerve and arrowroot powder slowly. Continue to mix until the meringue mixture begins to form and pulls away from the sides of the bowl.

Spoon 18 circles onto the baking sheet.

Bake for 20 minutes.

Remove from oven and gently top with sliced almonds. Return to the oven and bake for an additional 20 minutes.

Allow to cool before removing from baking sheet.

# PEANUT BUTTER COOKIES

PREP TIME 10 MINUTES | COOK TIME 10 MINUTES | MAKES 24

1 cup creamy peanut butter

⅓ cup granulated monk fruit sweetener

½ teaspoon baking soda

1 large egg

⅓ cup chopped peanuts

Pinch of salt

---

Calories per serving 78
Total fat 7g
Total carbohydrates 3g
Fiber 1g; *Net carbs 2g*
Protein 4g

## Directions

Preheat oven to 350°F. Line a baking sheet with parchment.

Combine peanut butter, monk fruit sweetener, baking soda and egg with an electric mixer. Add the peanuts and mix well.

Roll the dough into 1½-inch balls and place them on the baking sheet. Press down gently with a fork in one direction, and then the opposite direction.

Bake for 8 to 10 minutes until the bottoms begin to brown. Let the cookies cool for 5 minutes on the baking sheet before moving to a cooling rack.

Bake in batches of 12 until you have used all the dough (keep the dough in the refrigerator between batches).

Store in an airtight container and keep refrigerated.

# PECAN SANDIES

PREP TIME 10 MINUTES | COOK TIME 15 MINUTES | SERVES 24

¾ cup almond flour

¼ cup coconut flour

1 large egg

4 tablespoons butter, melted

½ cup granulated Swerve

1 teaspoon vanilla extract

½ teaspoon baking powder

¼ teaspoon arrowroot powder

⅓ cup crushed pecans

---

Calories per serving 50
Total fat 4g
Total carbohydrates 7g
Fiber 1g; *Net carbs 6g*
Protein 1g

## Directions

Combine dry ingredients, mixing until well combined.

In a separate bowl add melted butter and vanilla extract. Slowly add half of the dry ingredients and mix using an electric mixer.

Add the egg and the remaining dry ingredients. Continue to mix until well combined.

Fold in the crushed pecans until dispersed evenly throughout the batter.

Pour the dough onto a large piece of parchment paper. Form the dough into a log and roll it up with the parchment paper. Freeze for 30 minutes.

Preheat the oven to 350°F. Line a baking sheet with parchment paper.

Remove from the freezer and slice into ¼-inch thick cookies.

Bake for 15 minutes or until golden brown.

Allow to cool for at least 20 minutes before handling to prevent the cookies from falling apart.

Store in an airtight container for up to 10 days.

# VANILLA SHORTBREAD COOKIES

PREP TIME 10 MINUTES | COOK TIME 15 MINUTES | MAKES 16

6 tablespoons butter

2 cups almond flour

⅓ cup monk fruit sweetener

1 teaspoon vanilla extract

---

Calories per serving 123
Total fat 11g
Total carbohydrates 3g
Fiber 2g; *Net carbs 2g*
Protein 3g

## Directions

Melt butter in a small saucepan on low heat.

Combine almond flour, monk fruit sweetener, and vanilla extract.

Slowly stir in the melted butter slowly and mix until combined fully.

Mold the dough into a log shape and wrap with plastic wrap .

Refrigerate for 2 hours.

Preheat oven to 350°F. Line a baking sheet with parchment paper.

Cut the log into ½-inch thick slices and place on baking sheet.

Bake for 15 minutes, or until golden brown.

Allow to cool and serve.

# NO-BAKE COOKIES

2 tablespoons butter, melted

⅔ cup almond butter

1 cup unsweetened shredded coconut

4 drops of vanilla stevia

⅓ cup chopped pecans

Calories per serving 106
Total fat 10g
Total carbohydrates 3g
Fiber 2g; *Net carbs 1g*
Protein 1g

## Directions

Line a tray with parchment paper.

Mix all ingredients in a large bowl until well combined.

Drop 2-inch spoonfuls of dough on to the lined tray.

Freeze for 10 to 15 minutes.

Store in an airtight container in the refrigerator until ready to eat.

# MACADAMIA BISCOTTI

PREP TIME 10 MINUTES | COOK TIME 15 MINUTES | MAKES 16

¾ cup superfine almond flour

⅓ cup Swerve Confectioners

1 teaspoon baking powder

1 teaspoon arrowroot powder

½ teaspoon almond extract

⅓ dry-roasted macadamia nuts

⅓ cup salted butter, melted

2 large eggs

---

Calories per serving 93
Total fat 9g
Total carbohydrates 7g
Fiber 1g; **Net carbs 6g**
Protein 2g

## Directions

Preheat oven to 325°F. Line a baking sheet with parchment paper.

Combine almond flour, Confectioners Swerve, baking powder, arrowroot powder, almond extract and macadamia nuts. Mix until well combined.

In a separate bowl beat the melted butter and eggs.

Slowly add egg mixture to dry ingredients, mixing until a dough forms.

Transfer dough to a clean, dry work surface. Form the dough an even, slightly flattened, rectangle shaped log. (the dough is sticky. To help with the shaping, dust your hands with almond flour).

Place dough on baking sheet and bake for 30 minutes or until firm and golden brown. Remove from oven and allow to cool for about 15 minutes.

Preheat oven to 250°F.

Slice loaf into ½-inch thick slices. (if your loaf is crumbly and wont slice, freeze it for a few minutes to firm it up).

Line slices on baking sheet and bake for 15 minutes. Flip and bake for an additional 15 minutes.

Turn oven off and allow biscotti to cool in the oven until crisp.

Store in an airtight container.

# FAT BOMBS

# CHOCOLATY FAT BOMBS

PREP TIME 15 MINUTES | COOK TIME 1 HOUR | MAKES 30 BOMBS

1 cup almond butter

1 cup coconut oil

1/2 cup unsweetened cocoa powder

1/3 cup coconut flour

1/4 teaspoon stevia or 1-2 teaspoons monk fruit sweetener

A pinch of salt

---

Calories per serving 75
Total fat 8g
Total carbohydrates 2g
Fiber 1g; **Net carbs 1g**
Protein 1g

## Directions

In a small saucepan over medium heat, melt and combine the almond butter and coconut oil.

In the same pot, add the dry ingredients and mix until well-combined.

Pour the mixture into a bowl and place in the freezer for about 45 minutes.

Once your mixture has set, remove the bowl from the freezer and form it into balls (coat your hands in a little bit of coconut oil, so the mixture doesn't stick to your hands).

Place the balls onto a tray or plate and return them to the freezer for 15 to 20 minutes.

# LEMON COCONUT FAT BOMBS

PREP TIME 10 MINUTES | MAKES 30 BOMBS

8 ounces cream cheese, room temperature

½ cup salted butter, room temperature

2 lemons

⅓ cup unsweetened shredded coconut

4 drops liquid stevia

---

Calories per serving 63
Total fat 6g
Total carbohydrates 1g
Fiber 0g; **Net carbs 1g**
Protein 1g

## Directions

Mix butter, cream cheese, shredded coconut, and stevia with an electric mixer until smooth. Add the zest of 1 lemon, and juice of both lemons. Mix until well combined.

Spoon the mixture into silicone molds or mini-muffin liners. Freeze until the fat bombs are firm.

Remove from the molds and keep frozen in an airtight container until ready to serve.

Calories per serving 116
Total fat 12g
Total carbohydrates 1g
Fiber 1g; *Net carbs 1g*
Protein 2g

# CINNAMON ROLL FAT BOMBS

PREP TIME 15 MINUTES | MAKES 24 BOMBS

## Fat bombs:

8 ounces cream cheese, softened

½ cup butter, softened

½ cup smooth almond butter

½ cup golden monk fruit sweetener

2 teaspoons gorund cinnamon

1 teaspoon vanilla extract

¼ cup finely chopped walnuts

## Frosting:

1 tablespoon heavy whipping cream

1 ½ ounces cream cheese, softened

2 teaspoons golden monk fruit sweetener

¼ teaspoon vanilla extract

## Directions

Using a stand mixer (or an electric mixer), mix all fat bomb ingredients until well combined.

Refrigerate mixture for 30 minutes.

Form the mixture into balls, place them on a tray lined with parchment paper and freeze for 45 minutes.

Make the frosting by combining all ingredients until smooth.

Drizzle on top of the fat bombs and serve.

# COOKIE DOUGH FAT BOMBS

PREP TIME 10 MINUTES | COOK TIME 40 MINUTES | MAKES 12 BOMBS

6 tablespoon softened butter

6 ounces cream cheese

3 tablespoon stevia

6 scoops powdered mct powder

1 teaspoon vanilla extract

½ cup almond butter

¼ cup low sugar chocolate chips

Calories per serving 191
Total fat 23g
Total carbohydrates 1g
Fiber 0g; *Net carbs 1g*
Protein 1g

## Directions

Combine the butter, cream cheese, vanilla extract, stevia, mct powder, and almond butter in a bowl using a hand mixer or stand mixer. Mix until they are well incorporated.

Stir in the chocolate chips, then cover and freeze for about 10 minutes.

Remove the bowl from the freezer and use a spoon or ice cream scoop to scoop the cookie dough onto a wax paper, lined dish. Place the dough balls back in the freezer for 20 to 30 minutes or until firm.

When they're completely frozen, remove the "cookies" from the freezer and place in a resealable plastic bag or airtight container. Store them in the freezer until you are ready to eat.

# PEPPERMINT PATTY FAT BOMBS

PREP TIME 10 MINUTES | MAKES 24 BOMBS

2 teaspoons peppermint extract

½ cup coconut oil, solid

3 tablespoons finely shredded unsweetened coconut

2 tablespoons Swerve sweetener

¼ cup heavy cream

⅛ teaspoon sea salt

Chocolate layer:

2 ½ tablespoons unsweetened cocoa powder

2 tablespoons butter

1 tablespoon heavy cream

¾ cup raw cocoa butter

Calories per serving 119
Total fat 13g
Total carbohydrates 1g
Fiber 0g; *Net carbs 0g*
Protein 0g

## Directions

Line a baking sheet with parchment paper.

Mix peppermint extract, coconut oil, shredded coconut, Swerve sweetener, sea salt, and heavy cream with a hand mixer until mixture turns into a paste.

Spoon the mixture into a silicone mold. Freeze until solid, about 1 to 2 hours.

Melt the chocolate layer ingredients in a saucepan over low heat, stirring frequently.

Remove silicone mold from freezer and pop out coconut fat bombs.

Using a fork, carefully dunk the fat bombs into the melted chocolate and place on baking sheet. Allow to harden in freezer.

Once chocolate has hardened, remove from freezer and serve.

# CACAO CASHEW FAT BOMBS

PREP TIME 15 MINUTES | COOK TIME 5 MINUTES | MAKES 20 BOMBS

1 cup coconut oil

1 cup almond butter

¼ cup coconut flour

½ cup cacao powder

1 cup raw cashews

¼ teaspoon salt

Calories per serving 149
Total fat 15g
Total carbohydrates 4g
Fiber 2g; *Net carbs 3g*
Protein 2g

## Directions

Melt coconut oil and almond butter over a medium heat.

Transfer into a bowl. Stir in coconut flour and cacao powder, mixing until well combined.

Freeze for about 15 minutes until mixture is solid.

Lightly pulse the cashews in a food processor until finely chopped.

Remove fat bomb mixture from freezer and scoop a ½ tablespoon of the mixture into your hand.
Roll into a ball and coat with the blended cashews.

Refrigerate until solid and serve.

# CHOCOLATE HAZELNUT FAT BOMBS

PREP TIME 5 MINUTES | COOK TIME 5 MINUTES | MAKES 8 BOMBS

½ cup unsweetened cocoa butter

½ cup roasted hazelnuts, chopped

1 tablespoon unsweetened cocoa powder

2 tablespoons monk fruit sweetener

¼ teaspoon hazelnut extract

Pinch of salt

Calories per serving 56
Total fat 4g
Total carbohydrates 8g
Fiber 4g; **Net carbs 3g**
Protein 3g

## Directions

In a saucepan over low heat, melt the cocoa butter.

Add chopped hazelnuts, cocoa powder, monk fruit sweetener, hazelnut extract and salt, stirring constantly.

Slowly pour the mixture into silicone molds or an ice cube tray.

Freeze for at least 1 hour before serving.

# CASHEW BUTTER FAT BOMBS

PREP TIME 5 MINUTES | COOK TIME 5 MINUTES | MAKES 12 BOMBS

6 tablespoons cashew butter

6 tablespoons butter

1 teaspoon vanilla extract

½ teaspoon monk fruit sweetener

Pinch of sea salt

Calories per serving 99
Total fat 10g
Total carbohydrates 2g
Fiber 0g; *Net carbs 2g*
Protein 2g

## Directions

Line a mini muffin tin with paper liners.

Melt cashew butter and butter in a saucepan over low heat, stirring until well combined.

Add remaining ingredients, stirring well.

Evenly spoon the mixture evenly into muffin tin.

Freeze for at least 1 hour before serving.

# PUMPKIN SPICE FAT BOMBS

PREP TIME 10 MINUTES | COOK TIME 5 MINUTES | MAKES 24 BOMBS

½ cup pecans

½ cup coconut oil

4 ounces cream cheese

½ cup pumpkin puree

¼ cup monk fruit sweetener

½ teaspoon ground nutmeg

¼ teaspoon ground cloves

1 teaspoon ground cinnamon

---

Calories per serving 58
Total fat 6g
Total carbohydrates 1g
Fiber 0g; *Net carbs 1g*
Protein 0g

## Directions

Toast pecans in a small skillet over medium heat until slightly browned. Remove from heat and set aside.

Melt coconut oil and cream cheese in a saucepan on low heat (make sure to keep the temperature low so it does not burn).

Combine cream cheese mixture, pumpkin puree, monk fruit sweetener and spices. Beat with an electric mixer until well combined.

Spoon mixture into silicone mold and top with 1 to 2 toasted pecans. Dust with additional cinnamon if desired.

Freeze for about 4 hours until solid.

Remove from mold and serve.

# LEMON MACADAMIA FAT BOMBS

PREP TIME 5 MINUTES | COOK TIME 10 MINUTES | MAKES 30 BOMBS

¾ cup coconut oil

5 tablespoons coconut cream

3 tablespoons superfine almond flour

3 tablespoons coconut flour

¼ teaspoon vanilla extract

Juice and zest from 1 lemon

Liquid stevia to taste

½ cup unsweetened finely shredded coconut

½ cup chopped macadamia nuts

Pinch of salt

Calories per serving 86
Total fat 16g
Total carbohydrates 2g
Fiber 1g; *Net carbs 1g*
Protein 1g

## Directions

Melt coconut oil and coconut cream in a saucepan over a low heat.

Whisk in coconut and almond flour, vanilla extract, lemon juice, lemon zest, stevia, and salt. Mix until well combined and smooth.

Remove from heat and stir in shredded coconut and chopped macadamia nuts until distributed evenly.

Pour evenly into silicone molds or an ice cube tray. Freeze until firm and serve.

# BUTTER PECAN FAT BOMBS

PREP TIME 2 MINUTES | COOK TIME 5 MINUTES | MAKES 12 BOMBS

½ cup pecans

¼ cup coconut butter

¼ cup butter

¼ cup coconut oil

½ teaspoon vanilla extract

¼ cup granulated Swerve

⅛ teaspoon sea salt

---

Calories per serving 175
Total fat 19g
Total carbohydrates 3g
Fiber 2g; *Net carbs 1g*
Protein 1g

## Directions

In a skillet over medium heat, toast pecans until they are golden brown. Cool before chopping roughly.

Melt coconut butter, butter and coconut oil in a saucepan over low heat.

Stir in vanilla extract, sea salt, and Swerve and mix well.

Divide the chopped pecans into 12 silicone molds.

Evenly pour melted butter and coconut mixture evenly over the pecans.

Freeze for at least 1 hour or until hardened.

Remove from silicone tray and serve.

Store remaining fat bombs in the freezer.

# ALMOND PISTACHIO FAT BOMBS

PREP TIME 15 MINUTES | COOK TIME 4 MINUTES | MAKES 36 BOMBS

½ cup cacao butter, melted

1 cup smooth almond butter

1 cup coconut butter

1 cup coconut oil, hardened

½ cup full-fat coconut milk

¼ cup ghee

1 tablespoon vanilla extract

1 teaspoon cinnamon

¼ teaspoon ground cloves

¼ teaspoon ground nutmeg

¼ teaspoon almond extract

¼ teaspoon sea salt

¼ cup raw shelled pistachios, chopped

---

Calories per serving 156
Total fat 16g
Total carbohydrates 3g
Fiber 2g; **Net carbs 1g**
Protein 2g

## Directions

Lightly grease a 9x9-inch baking dish and line with parchment paper.

Melt the cacao butter in a small saucepan set over low heat, stirring often.

Mix all of the ingredients except for cacao butter and shelled pistachios with an electric mixer in a large bowl.

Pour the melted cacao butter into the almond mixture and resume mixing on low speed until well incorporated.

Transfer to prepared dish, spread as evenly as possible. Sprinkle with chopped pistachios.

Refrigerate until completely set, at least 4 hours but preferably overnight.

Cut into 36 squares and serve.

# GINGER SPICE FAT BOMBS

PREP TIME 10 MINUTES | COOK TIME 2 MINUTES | MAKES 16 BOMBS

2 cups superfine almond flour

⅔ cup monk fruit sweetener

1 teaspoon ground ginger

½ teaspoon ground cinnamon

½ teaspoon ground nutmeg

¼ teaspoon sea salt

6 tablespoons butter, melted

---

Calories per serving 124
Total fat 11g
Total carbohydrates 3g
Fiber 2g; *Net carbs 2g*
Protein 3g

## Directions

Line a tray with parchment paper.

Add all of the dry ingredients to a medium-sized bowl, mixing well.

Stir in melted butter to form a thick dough.

Using a small ice cream scoop, scoop dough and roll it into balls.

Place the balls on parchment lined tray and freeze for at least 1 hour before serving.

Store fat bombs in an airtight container in the freezer or refrigerator.

# MATCHA COCONUT FAT BOMBS

PREP TIME 15 MINUTES | MAKES 32 BOMBS

Fat bombs:

1 cup coconut oil, hardened

1 cup coconut butter

½ cup full-fat coconut cream

½ teaspoon unsweetened matcha green tea powder

¼ teaspoon sea salt

1 teaspoon vanilla extract

Coating:

1 cup finely shredded unsweetened coconut

1 tablespoon unsweetened matcha green tea powder

## Directions

Combine all of the fat bomb ingredients with an electric mixer until light and fluffy.

Refrigerate for about an hour until the mixture hardens slightly.

Combine the shredded coconut and matcha powder.

Using a small ice cream scoop, scoop the fat bomb mixture into 32 balls.

Roll the balls quickly in your hands and place in the coating. Roll in the coating until evenly covered.

Store in an airtight container in the refrigerator for up to 2 weeks.

Calories per serving 123
Total Fat 13g
Total Carbohydrates 2g;
Fiber 2g; *Net Carbs 1g*
Protein 1g

# BARS & BITES

# FUDGY BROWNIES

PREP TIME 5 MINUTES | COOK TIME 40 MINUTES | SERVES 8

6 eggs

1 ½ sticks of butter

4 ounces cream cheese, room temperature

5 tablespoons unsweetened cocoa powder

½ teaspoon baking powder

2 tablespoons monk fruit sweetener

¼ teaspoon salt

---

Calories per serving 257
Total fat 3g
Total carbohydrates 1g
Fiber 2g; *Net carbs 2g*
Protein 6g

## Directions

Preheat oven to 350°F. Grease an 8x8-inch baking dish.

Mix all ingredients with an electric mixer until combined.

Bake for 40 minutes, or until a knife inserted into the center comes out clean.

Allow to cool slightly, cut, and serve.

Calories per serving 29
Total fat 2g
Total carbohydrates 7g
Fiber 1g; *Net carbs 7g*
Protein 1g

# LEMON-GLAZED SPICE FRITTERS

PREP TIME 10 MINUTES | COOK TIME 20 MINUTES | MAKES 14

## Fritters:

½ cup almond flour

3 tablespoons monk fruit sweetener, or stevia sweetener

1 teaspoon baking powder

1 large egg

½ teaspoon arrowroot powder

½ teaspoon cinnamon

¼ teaspoon nutmeg

½ teaspoon vanilla extract

Zest of half a lemon

2 cups refined coconut oil for frying

## Lemon Glaze:

2 tablespoons lemon juice

3 tablespoons Confectioners Swerve

## Directions

In a large bowl, mix all of the dry ingredients together.

Add the egg and mix until a sticky dough forms.

On the stove or in a deep fryer, heat the coconut oil to 375°F.

Drop balls of dough into the oil 4 or 5 at a time.

Allow the dough to brown on one side then rotate to the other side.

Cooking will take approximately 2 minutes per side.

Remove the fritter from the oil and set on paper towels to drain excess oil.

In a small bowl combine the lemon juice and Confetioners Swerve. Mix thoroughly until smooth.

Dip cooled fritters in icing and serve.

# COCONUT LIME BARS

PREP TIME 10 MINUTES | COOK TIME 25 MINUTES | MAKES 16

## Crust:

6 tablespoons salted butter

1 ½ cups superfine almond flour

½ cup unsweetened shredded coconut

⅓ cup granulated Swerve

¼ teaspoon vanilla extract

## Directions

Crust:

Preheat oven to 350°F and line an 8x8-inch baking dish.

Combine all of the crust ingredients in a bowl. Mix well until a dough forms.

Press the dough into the baking dish and about ½-inch up the sides.

Bake for 10 minutes.

Allow to cool while you make the filling.

## Filling:

Melt butter in a saucepan over a low heat.

Remove from heat and whisk in Swerve, lime juice and lime zest.

Slowly add in the egg yolks and continue to whisk.

Return to the stove and cook over low heat, continually whisking until the curd begins to thicken.

Remove from heat. Whisk in arrowroot powder and gelatin until completely dissolved.

Pour filling over the crust and spread evenly.

Bake for 15 minutes.

When cooled, cut into squares and garnish with additional lime zest or shredded coconut, and serve.

## Filling:

½ cup salted butter

⅔ cup granulated Swerve

½ cup fresh lime juice

¼ cup grated lime zest

6 egg yolks

¼ teaspoon arrowroot powder

1 tablespoon unflavored gelatin

---

Calories per serving 196
Total fat 19g
Total carbohydrates 4g
Fiber 2g; *Net carbs 2g*
Protein 4g

# LEMON BARS

PREP TIME 10 MINUTES | COOK TIME 20 MINUTES | MAKES 16

## Crust:

1 cup almond flour

2 tablespoons coconut flour

¼ cup granulated Swerve

¾ cup butter

1 egg yolk

¼ teaspoon salt

½ teaspoon vanilla extract

## Directions

Preheat oven to 350°F. Line a 8x8-inch baking dish with parchment paper.

Melt butter in a saucepan over medium heat. Once melted pour into a large bowl. Add the Swerve, vanilla extract, and egg yolk. Whisk until well combined.

Slowly add almond flour, coconut flour and salt. Continue mixing until dough forms.

Press dough evenly into bottom of baking dish and bake for 20 minutes.

Allow to cool while you make the filling.

Beat together the eggs, lemon juice, lemon zest, and Swerve with an electric mixer.

Add arrowroot powder and mix until well combined.

Pour filling over crust and bake for 20 minutes or until filling has set.

Allow to cool completely and refrigerate for 1 hour.

Slice into 16 bars and serve.

Filling:

½ cup granulated Swerve

4 large eggs

⅔ cup fresh lemon juice

2 tablespoons lemon zest

1 tablespoon arrowroot powder

Calories per serving 149
Total fat 14g
Total carbohydrates 3g
Fiber 1g; *Net carbs 2g*
Protein 4g

# PUMPKIN CHEESECAKE BARS

PREP TIME 30 MINUTES | COOK TIME 1 HOUR 5 MINUTES | MAKES 24

## Crust:

2 cups superfine almond flour

6 tablespoons salted butter

2 tablespoons granulated Swerve

## Directions

Preheat oven to 300°F. Line a 9x13-inch baking dish with parchment paper.

Melt butter and pour into a large bowl. Add Swerve and mix until well combined.

Slowly add in almond flour, mixing until a dough forms.

Press the dough evenly into the bottom of the baking dish. Bake for 15 minutes.

Allow to cool while you make the filling.

Heat oven to 350°F.

Using a hand mixer, cream together the cream cheese, salt, and granulated Swerve together.

Add eggs one at a time, beating until well combined.

Add pumpkin, cinnamon, cloves, and nutmeg, beating until light and fluffy.

Spread the filling over the crust evenly using a spatula.

Bake for 50 minutes. Allow to cool completely.

Refrigerate for 8 hours or overnight, allowing the cheesecake to set fully.

Slice into bars and serve.

Filling:

32 ounces cream cheese, room temperature

1 ½ cups granulated swerve sweetener

4 large eggs

8 ounces organic canned pumpkin

1 teaspoon ground cinnamon

¼ teaspoon ground nutmeg

⅛ teaspoon ground cloves

⅛ teaspoon salt

Calories per serving 223
Total fat 22
Total carbohydrates 4g
Fiber 1g; *Net carbs 3g*
Protein 6g

# PECAN PIE CLUSTERS

PREP TIME 5 MINUTES | COOK TIME 10 MINUTES | MAKES 10

1 cup chopped pecans

2 ounces dark chocolate, chopped

3 tablespoons salted butter

¼ cup heavy cream

2 tablespoons monk fruit sweetner

1 teaspoon vanilla extract

---

Calories per serving 156
Total fat 15g
Total carbohydrates 5g
Fiber 1g; *Net carbs 4g*
Protein 2g

## Directions

Line a baking sheet with parchment paper and set aside.

Over medium heat, melt butter until bubbling and golden brown.

Once golden, add heavy cream and slowly whisk. Reduce heat and simmer.

Add monk fruit sweetener and vanilla extract, whisking vigorously.

Continue whisking occasionally as mixture begins to thicken.

Remove from heat when mixture has a caramel-like consistency.

Mix in chopped pecans and spoon small clusters onto baking sheet

Freeze for 5 minutes

Over a double boiler, melt chocolate. Drizzle over clusters generously.

Store in refrigerator in an airtight container for up to 2 weeks.

# MOCHA CHEESECAKE FUDGE

16 ounces cream cheese, room temperature

1 cup salted butter, room temperature

⅓ cup granulated Swerve

2 tablespoons unsweetened cocoa powder

3 tablespoons cold brew coffee

¼ teaspoon vanilla extract

---

Calories per serving 202
Total fat 22g
Total carbohydrates 6g
Fiber 0g; **Net carbs 6g**
Protein 2g

## Directions

Line a 8x8-inch baking dish with parchment paper.

Combine butter, cream cheese, and Swerve with an electric mixer.

Scoop out 1 cup of cream cheese mixture and put it in a small bowl.

Add cocoa powder and mix well.

Add cold brew coffee to the remaining mixture. Mix until smooth.

Pour the cocoa mixture into the bottom of the baking dish and spread evenly.

Pour the coffee mixture on top of the cocoa mixture.

Freeze for 4 hours

Cut into 16 squares and serve. Store in an airtight container in the refrigerator.

# NO-BAKE CHOCOLATE
## COCONUT BARS

PREP TIME 5 MINUTES | MAKES 16

1 cup almond butter

1 ¼ cups sugar-free chocolate chips

1 tablespoon monk fruit sweetener

½ cup unrefined coconut oil

1 ½ cups unsweetened shredded coconut + some for topping

1 cup raw almonds, chopped

1 cup walnuts, chopped

1 cup unsalted roasted cashews, chopped

1 teaspoon vanilla extract

### Directions

Line an 8x8-inch baking dish with parchment paper.

Combine almond butter, coconut oil, chocolate chips, and monk fruit sweetener in a saucepan over a low heat. Stir frequently until smooth.

Add the remaining ingredients, mixing well.

Pour into baking dish. Top with additional shredded coconut.

Refrigerate for about 4 hours until the chocolate hardens.

Slice into square pieces and store in an airtight container.

Calories per serving 302
Total fat 29g
Total carbohydrates 8g
Fiber 2g; *Net carbs 6g*
Protein 5g

# MAGIC COOKIE BARS

PREP TIME 20 MINUTES | COOK TIME 60 MINUTES | MAKES 16

Cracker base:

1 cup almond flour

¼ teaspoon baking powder

1 egg

2 tablespoons salted butter

¼ teaspoon salt


Caramel sauce:

½ cup Swerve

½ cup butter

½ cup heavy cream

½ teaspoon vanilla extract

¼ teaspoon salt

## Directions

Preheat oven to 300°F.

Mix almond flour, salt and baking powder with an electric mixer. Add the egg and melted butter and mix until combined thoroughly.

Transfer the dough onto a large piece of parchment paper and flatten into a rough square.

Place another piece of parchment paper on top and roll out to ⅛-inch thick. Remove the top parchment paper.

Place the dough on large baking sheet and bake for 35 minutes, or until lightly browned. Remove from the oven and let cool. Increase oven temperature to 375°F.

While the crust is cooling make the caramel sauce.

Melt the butter in a saucepan over medium heat. Whisk in Swerve sweetener. Bring to a boil for 5 to 7 minutes, stirring constantly until the mixture starts to darken.

Remove from the heat and whisk in the heavy cream and vanilla extract slowly.

Remove the parchment paper from the crust, and place it into a square pan. You may have to break some of the edges.

Pour half of the caramel sauce over the crust, spreading evenly.

Layer the cacao nibs, pecans, and shredded coconut. Drizzle the remaining caramel sauce on top.

Bake for 5 minutes.

Cut into squares and store in an airtight container for up to a week.

Topping:

2 cups cacao nibs

1 cup chopped pecans

1 cup unsweetened shredded coconut

Calories per serving 197
Total fat 18g
Total carbohydrates 13g
Fiber 3g; *Net carbs 10g*
Protein 3g

# SALTED CARAMEL PECAN BRITTLE

PREP TIME 5 MINUTES | COOK TIME 7 MINUTES | MAKES 8

1 cup chopped pecans

¼ cup salted butter

⅓ cup golden monk fruit sweetener

2 teaspoons vanilla extract

⅛ teaspoon coarse sea salt

---

Calories per serving 149
Total fat 16g
Total carbohydrates 2g
Fiber 2g; *Net carbs 1g*
Protein 2g

## Directions

Line a 9x9-inch baking dish with parchment paper.

Melt butter, monk fruit sweetener, and vanilla extract in a non-stick skillet over medium heat until sweetener is dissolved.

Add the pecans and allow to boil for 2 to 3 minutes until mixture turns a light brown color.

Pour mixture into baking dish carefully and spread pecans evenly with the back of a spoon.

Sprinkle with coarse sea salt.

Allow to cool completely until solid all the way through.

Break into pieces and store in an airtight container for up to 2 weeks.

# SALTED TOFFEE NUT CUPS

PREP TIME 15 MINUTES | MAKES 5

5 ounces sugar free dark chocolate

3 ½ tablespoons monk fruit sweetener

3 tablespoons butter

½ ounce raw walnuts, chopped

Sea salt to taste

Calories per serving 191
Total fat 17g
Total carbohydrates 18g
Fiber 3g; *Net carbs 15g*
Protein 2g

## Directions

Prepare a double boiler. Melt chocolate until smooth.

Line a cupcake pan with 5 paper liners.

Drop a spoonful of chocolate into each liner and spread evenly on the bottom (keep some chocolate to the top of the toffee nut cups).

Freeze to harden.

Combine butter and monk fruit sweetener in a saucepan over a medium heat, stirring until sweetener is completely dissolved completely.

Once the mixture starts to thicken, add the chopped walnuts.

Remove the chocolate cups from the freezer and fill each cup with a half spoon full of toffee mixture, working quickly before the toffee hardens.

Drizzle remaining melted chocolate on top and sprinkle with sea salt.

Freeze for an additional hour and serve.

# CACAO BUTTER BLONDIES

PREP TIME 15 MINUTES | COOK TIME 30 MINUTES | MAKES 20

6 tablespoons unsweetened cacao butter

4 tablespoons salted butter

2 eggs

½ cup monk fruit sweetener

½ teaspoon almond extract

2 tablespoons coconut cream

¼ cup superfine almond flour

2 tablespoons coconut flour

¼ teaspoon baking soda

½ cup cacao nibs

2 tablespoons pecans

---

Calories per serving 51
Total fat 4g
Total carbohydrates 2g
Fiber 1g; **Net carbs 1g**
Protein 1g

## Directions

Preheat oven to 325°F. Line an 8-inch baking dish with parchment paper.

In a small pan melt the cacao butter and salted butter until there are no lumps. Allow to cool slightly.

Mix eggs, monk fruit sweetener and almond extract with an electric mixer. Slowly add the coconut cream.

Add the cooled butter mixture. Mix until smooth and creamy.

In a separate bowl combine dry ingredients, then add to the wet ingredients. Mix well.

Add the cacao nibs and pecans and mix one last time.

Pour dough into the baking dish and spread evenly.

Bake for 30 minutes or until a toothpick inserted into the center comes out clean.

Allow to cool completely before serving.

# PEANUT BUTTER CHEESECAKE BITES

PREP TIME 15 MINUTES | COOK TIME 5 MINUTES | MAKES 12

½ cup peanut butter, unsweetened

8 ounces cream cheese, softened

¼ cup monk fruit sweetener

1 teaspoon vanilla extract

100g dark chocolate

1 tablespoon coconut oil

---

Calories per serving 184
Total fat 16g
Total carbohydrates 8g
Fiber 1g; *Net carbs 7g*
Protein 5g

## Directions

Line a baking tray with parchment paper.

Beat the peanut butter, Swerve, monk fruit sweetener, cream cheese and vanilla extract with a hand mixer.

Mold the mixture into 12 balls and place on the prepared tray.

Freeze for 1 hour until firm.

Prepare a double boiler. Melt the chocolate and mix in the coconut oil.

Dip each bite into the chocolate mixture.

Freeze for an additional 30 minutes or until the chocolate has hardened.

Store the freezer in an airtight container until you are ready to eat them.

# TOASTED COCONUT LEMON SQUARES

PREP TIME 15 MINUTES | COOK TIME 35 MINUTES | SERVES 12

## Crust:

1 cup almond flour

¼ cup coconut flour

¼ cup Swerve

½ tablespoon lemon zest

3 tablespoons butter, softened

## Filling:

¾ cup Swerve sweetener

1 tablespoon butter, softened

½ cup coconut milk

1 cup lemon juice

½ tablespoon lemon zest

5 large eggs

## Directions

Preheat oven to 350°F. Grease a 9x9-inch pan and set aside

Combine almond flour, coconut flour, Swerve, and lemon zest until combined thoroughly.

Add the melted butter, mixing with an electric mixer until a dough forms.

Press the dough into the baking dish and bake for 15 minutes or until crust is golden.

Allow to cool while you make the filling.

Combine butter, Swerve sweetener, lemon zest and coconut milk over a medium heat. Stir until the sweetener is dissolved completely.

Add lemon juice and slowly whisk in the eggs until the mixture has thickened.

Pour the filling into the crust and bake for 15 minutes.

In a food processor, pulse the toasted coconut, almond flour and butter until well combined and crumbly.

Sprinkle topping on lemon squares and bake for an additional 5 minutes to crisp the top.

Cool before cutting and serving.

Topping:

¾ cup toasted coconut chips, unsweetened

2 tablespoons almond flour

½ tablespoon butter

Calories per serving 169
Total fat 14g
Total carbohydrates 5g
Fiber 3g; *Net carbs 3g*
Protein 6g

# SMOOTH & CREAMY

# CHOCOLATE MILKSHAKE

½ cup heavy cream

½ medium avocado

2 tablespoons unsweetened cocoa powder

½ teaspoon vanilla extract

3 tablespoons monk fruit sweetener

½ cup ice

---

Calories per serving 443
Total fat 43g
Total carbohydrates 16g
Fiber 10g; *Net carbs 6g*
Protein 5g

## Directions

Add ingredients into a high-powered blender.

Blend until smooth and creamy.

Pour into a glass and serve.

# VANILLA BEAN MILKSHAKE

1 cup full-fat coconut cream

1 fresh vanilla bean

½ teaspoon vanilla extract

3 tablespoons monk fruit sweetener

½ cup ice cubes

Calories per serving 529
Total fat 52g
Total carbohydrates 8g
Fiber 0g; *Net carbs 8g*
Protein 4g

## Directions

Add coconut cream, vanilla extract, monk fruit sweetener, and ice to a high powered blender.

Scrape vanilla bean pod and add seeds to blender.

Blend until smooth and creamy.

Pour into a glass and serve.

# CHOCOLATE MOUSSE

PREP TIME 15 MINUTES | SERVES 8

8 ounces cream cheese, softened

¼ cup unsweetened cocoa powder

½ large avocado

⅛ teaspoon salt

⅛ teaspoon vanilla extract

3 drops liquid stevia

¼ cup heavy whipping cream

Calories per serving 145
Total fat 14g
Total carbohydrates 4g
Fiber 2g; **Net carbs 2g**
Protein 3g

Directions

Cream together the cream cheese and avocado with an electric mixer.

Slowly add in cocoa powder, vanilla extract, stevia and salt. Mix until well combined.

In a separate bowl, whip the heavy cream until stiff peaks form.

Fold the whipped cream into the chocolate mixture gently using a rubber spatula.

Chill for an hour before serving.

# CARAMEL SAUCE

⅓ cup salted butter

3 tablespoons granulated Swerve

⅔ cup heavy cream

1 teaspoon vanilla extract

---

Calories per 1 tablespoon 68
Total fat 8g
Total carbohydrates 0g
Fiber 0g; *Net carbs 0g*
Protein 0g

## Directions

In a saucepan over low heat, melt butter and Swerve Sweetener together until golden brown.

Whisk in the cream slowly and bring to a gentle boil. Reduce heat and simmer for 7 to 10 minutes, stirring occasionally until the caramel thickens enough to coat the back of a spoon.

Remove from heat, whisk in vanilla extract, and drizzle over your favorite treat.

# LEMON MERINGUE CUSTARD

PREP TIME 15 MINUTES | COOK TIME 5 MINUTES | SERVES 4

### Custard:

⅓ cup monk fruit sweetener

½ teaspoon arrowroot powder

Zest of 2 lemons

1 teaspoon lemon juice

1 ½ cups heavy cream

2 large egg yolks

½ teaspoon vanilla extract

⅛ teaspoon salt

### Directions

Heat heavy cream in a medium saucepan over low heat. Add monk fruit sweetener, arrowroot powder, salt and lemon zest, whisking well.

Whisk in the egg yolks. Increase heat to medium low. Continue whisking until the mixture begins to simmer.

Remove from heat. Add vanilla extract and lemon juice, mixing well.

Pour the custard into four 4-ounce ramekins and set aside.

For the meringue, whip egg whites and cream of tartar with an electric mixer until soft peaks form.

Add monk fruit sweetener and vanilla extract. Whip on high until stiff peaks form.

Spoon the meringue on top of the custard.

Turn broiler on high and place the top rack about 8-inches from the broiler.

Place ramekins under the broiler until the meringue is lightly browned (about 1 to 2 minutes, being careful not to burn the meringue).

Transfer ramekins to the refrigerator and chill for 2 hours before serving.

Meringue:

2 large egg whites, room temperature

⅛ teaspoon cream of tartar

1 tablespoon monk fruit sweetener

⅛ teaspoon vanilla extract

Calories per serving 201
Total fat 19g
Total carbohydrates 4g
Fiber 0g; *Net carbs 4g*
Protein 4g

# DECONSTRUCTED WAFFLE CONE

Ice cream:

4 large eggs

¼ teaspoon apple cider vinegar

½ cup granulated Swerve

1 ¼ cups heavy whipping cream

1 vanilla bean

Directions

Ice cream:

Separate the egg whites from yolks. Add apple cider vinegar and whisk until soft peaks begin to form.

Slowly add the granulated Swerve. Whisk until stiff peaks appear.

In a separate bowl, whip the heavy cream and vanilla bean until soft peaks form, being careful not to over whip.

In a third bowl, whisk the egg yolks.

Slowly fold the egg whites into the whipped cream slowly using a rubber spatula, then add the egg yolk mixture. Fold until well combined gently.

Place the mixture into a loaf pan and freeze for at least 2 hours.

Waffles:

Heat a waffle iron to high heat.

Combine the waffle ingredients and mix with an electric mixer until well combined.

Grease the waffle iron and place ¼ cup of the batter into the center of the iron and close. Cook until slightly crisp (about 4 minutes) and repeat with remaining batter.

Peanut butter sauce:

Combine peanut butter, melted butter, and granulated Swerve. Mix with an electric mixer until smooth.

To build your deconstructed waffle cone, place waffle in the bottom of a dish, add a scoop of ice cream, drizzle peanut butter sauce over the top, and serve.

Waffles:

1 cup almond flour

3 eggs

2 tablespoons unsweetened cocoa powder

½ teaspoon baking powder

⅛ teaspoon sea salt

1 tablespoon coconut oil

1 teaspoon almond extract

2 drops liquid stevia

Peanut butter sauce:

½ cup natural smooth peanut butter, room temperature

¼ cup butter, melted

¼ cup granulated Swerve

Calories per serving 880
Total fat 81g
Total carbohydrates 16g
Fiber 6g; *Net carbs 11g*
Protein 26g

# NO-CHURN FRENCH VANILLA ICE CREAM

PREP TIME 10 MINUTES | SERVES 6

4 large eggs

¼ teaspoon cream of tartar

½ cup monk fruit sweetener

1 ¼ cups heavy whipping cream

1 vanilla bean, scraped

½ teaspoon vanilla extract

⅛ teaspoon salt

---

Calories per serving 135
Total fat 12g
Total carbohydrates 1g
Fiber 0g; **Net carbs 1g**
Protein 5g

## Directions

Separate the egg whites from the egg yolks.

Whisk the egg whites and cream of tartar until soft peaks form.

Slowly add in the monk fruit sweetener and continue whisking until the peaks become stiff.

In a separate bowl, whip the heavy cream until soft peaks form.

In a third bowl, lightly whisk the egg yolks, seeds from vanilla bean, vanilla extract, and salt.

Fold the whisked egg whites into the whipped cream gently. Fold the egg yolk mixture into the whipped cream carefully until combined thoroughly.

Pour the ice cream into a loaf pan. Freeze for at least 2 hours before serving.

# COOKIES AND CREAM ICE CREAM

PREP TIME 20 MINUTES | COOK TIME 20 MINUTES | SERVES 1

Cookie crumbs:

¾ cup almond flour

¼ cup cocoa powder

¼ teaspoon baking soda

1 egg

¼ cup monk fruit sweetener

½ teaspoon vanilla extract

1 ½ tablespoons butter, softened

Pinch of salt

## Directions

Preheat oven to 300°F. Line 9-inch cake pan with parchment paper.

Mix almond flour, cocoa powder, baking soda, monk fruit sweetener and salt in a large bowl until well combined

Add the vanilla extract and butter. Continue mixing until dough forms into small crumbs.

Add the egg and mix until a dough begins to form.

Place the dough into cake pan and press until a thin layer evenly covers the bottom of the pan.

Bake for 20 minutes or until center of cookie bounces back when pressed. Remove pan from oven and allow to cool completely.

Once cooled, break into small crumbles and set aside.

Whip the whipping cream with an electric mixer until stiff peaks form.

Add vanilla extract and monk fruit sweetener, and whip until combined thoroughly (be careful to not over-whip).

Add coconut milk and blend until the mixture re-thickens.

Pour the mixture into an ice cream maker and churn.

Pour the cookie crumbles slowly into the ice cream maker. While it is churning to mix the crumbles evenly into the ice cream.

Remove ice cream and place in a ½-gallon freezer-safe container. Freeze for at least 2 hours before serving.

Ice Cream:

2 ½ cups heavy whipping cream

1 tablespoon vanilla extract

½ cup monk fruit sweetener

½ cup full fat coconut milk

---

Calories per serving 567
Total fat 58g
Total carbohydrates 21g
Fiber 4g; *Net carbs 17g*
Protein 8g

# NO-CHURN CHOCOLATE

## ALMOND ICE CREAM

PREP TIME 15 MINUTES | COOK TIME 5 MINUTES | SERVES 10

1 can of full-fat coconut milk

⅔ granulated monk fruit sweetener

¾ cup unsweetened cocoa powder

¼ teaspoon sea salt

¼ teaspoon arrowroot powder

1 teaspoon vanilla extract

2 cups heavy cream

2 tablespoons vodka (optional: this lowers the freezing point and prevents the ice cream from becoming too hard)

⅓ cup chopped almonds

---

Calories per serving 136
Total fat 13g
Total carbohydrates 7g
Fiber 3g; **Net carbs 5g**
Protein 3g

### Directions

Add coconut milk, monk fruit sweetener, cocoa and salt to a saucepan over medium heat. Whisk until the mixture is smooth.

Sprinkle arrowroot powder in slowly and continue whisking until fully combined and smooth. Remove from heat and allow the mixture to cool completely.

In a large bowl, whip heavy cream and vanilla extract until soft peaks form.

Add cooled cocoa mixture slowly and continue mixing until well combined.

Fold in the chopped almonds and vodka and mix until evenly combined.

Pour ice cream into a freezer safe container and freeze for at least 4 to 6 hours.

Allow to soften slightly if necessary, before serving.

# LEMON MOUSSE

PREP TIME 15 MINUTES | COOK TIME 5 MINUTES | SERVES 5

Mousse:

2 lemons, juiced and zested

4 eggs, separated

4 tablespoons full fat plain yogurt

5 tablespoons granulated Swerve

Whipped cream:

½ cup heavy whipping cream

¼ teaspoon vanilla extract

2 tablespoons granulated Swerve

---

Calories per serving 107
Total fat 8g
Total carbohydrates 18g
Fiber 1g; *Net carbs 18g*
Protein 5g

## Directions

Set up a double boiler with a glass bowl and add the egg yolks, lemon juice and lemon zest, Swerve, and yogurt

Whisk constantly until the mixture thickens into a curd like consistency.

Remove from the heat and set aside, stirring occasionally as it cools.

Whisk the egg whites until they form stiff peaks.

When the lemon curd mix has cooled completely, fold it into the egg whites gently until combined.

Pour mousse into ramekins and refrigerate for at least 2 hours.

In a medium bowl, beat the cream, vanilla extract, and Swerve until stiff peaks form.

Serve the mousse topped with a dollop of whipped cream.

# CINNAMON CHOCOLATE

## CHIA PUDDING

PREP TIME 5 MINUTES | SERVES 2

2 teaspoons unsweetened cocoa powder

1/2 teaspoon ground cinnamon

2 tablespoons chia seeds

1/3 cup coconut milk

1/8 teaspon vanilla extract

Stevia, to taste

Calories per serving 167
Total fat 14g
Total carbohydrates 10g
Fiber 7g; **Net carbs 3g**
Protein 4g

### Directions

I a bowl, combine cocoa powder, chia seeds, cinnamon, vanilla extract, and coconut milk.

Pour the chia mixture into 2 small jars or bowls.

Place in the refrigerator and let them set for 4 hours before serving.

# CHOCOLATE HAZELNUT SPREAD

PREP TIME 10 MINUTES | SERVES 1

1 cup hazelnuts, toasted and husked

4 tablespoons coconut oil, melted

2 tablespoons unsweetened cocoa powder

2 tablespoons confectioners swerve

½ teaspoon hazelnut extract

⅛ teaspoon salt

### Directions

In a food processor, blend hazelnuts until ground completely.

Add coconut oil, cocoa powder, Confectioners Swerve, hazelnut extract, and salt.

Mix until the mixture is smooth. If the mixture is too thick, add an additional tablespoon of coconut oil.

Store in a jar and keep refrigerated between uses.

Calories per serving 970
Total fat 102g
Total carbohydrates 49g
Fiber 11g; *Net carbs 38g*
Protein 14g

# GRASSHOPPER PIE MILKSHAKE

PREP TIME 5 MINUTES | SERVES 1

1 ripe avocado

1 cup full-fat coconut milk

⅓ cup heavy cream

½ cup ice cubes

⅛ teaspoon peppermint extract

Liquid stevia to taste (about 3-5 drops)

2 tablespoons raw cacao nibs

---

Calories per serving 1328
Total fat 122g
Total carbohydrates 54g
Fiber 24g; **Net carbs 31g**
Protein 15g

## Directions

Pit avocado and remove from skin.

Combine all ingredients in a high powered blender and blend until smooth and creamy.

Pour into a tall glass and top with additional cacao nibs, if desired, before serving.

# VANILLA PUDDING

PREP TIME 15 MINUTES | COOK TIME 12 MINUTES | SERVES 5

1 can of full-fat coconut milk

4 egg yolks

5 tablespoons arrowroot powder

1 ½ teaspoons vanilla extract

4 drops liquid stevia

---

Calories per serving 279
Total fat 22g
Total carbohydrates 14g
Fiber 0g; *Net carbs 14g*
Protein 4g

### Directions

Prepare a double boiler over medium heat. Whisk together egg yolks and arrowroot powder. Pour in coconut milk slowly, whisking until mixture thickens.

Remove from heat. Add vanilla extract and liquid stevia.

Pour mixture into a bowl, cover, and refrigerate overnight before serving.

# THANK YOU!

I hope you enjoyed making and eating the treats in this book as much as I enjoyed creating them. Be sure to head over to WarriorMade.com to get even more delicious Ketogenic recipes!

*Elisa Silva*

Chef Elisa